Designing Learning and Development for Return on Investment

Designing Learning and Development for Return on Investment

Carrie Foster

BEP BUSINESS EXPERT PRESS

Designing Learning and Development for Return on Investment
Copyright © Business Expert Press, LLC, 2017

First published in 2017 by
Business Expert Press, LLC
222 East 46th Street, New York, NY 10017
www.businessexpertpress.com

ISBN-13: 978-1-63157-742-0 (paperback)
ISBN-13: 978-1-63157-639-3 (e-book)

Business Expert Press Finance and Financial Management Collection

Collection ISSN: 2331-0049 (print)
Collection ISSN: 2331-0057 (electronic)

Cover and interior design by S4Carlisle Publishing Services
Private Ltd., Chennai, India

First edition: 2017

10 9 8 7 6 5 4 3 2 1

Printed in the United States of America.

Abstract

Learning practitioners have, for too long, been struggling to shift the perception of learning and development from a function that is a cost to the organization, to that of a function that is central to delivering value-added activities for the organization. The ability to deliver a return on investment is not about investing in good evaluation mechanisms, although this is important. It is imperative that the learning practitioner owns the numbers and works with financial metrics in order to bid for adequate resources and support the organization's strategic ambitions.

With an emphasis on the importance of designing Learning and Development *for* Return on Investment, this book offers a brief overview of both a theoretical and a practical framework. The theoretical underpinning provides an examination of how the theories and research about human and group dynamic processes and self-renewal can be utilized in intervention design. The emphasis is on the "self-renewal" ability of the individual and the facilitation of the movement of groups to improve the health and effectiveness of organizations in a sustainable way.

The book also offers a practical framework of two fundamentals of intervention design: the Diagnostic Phase—understanding the nature of the situation and the issues involved; and the Evaluation Phase—aligning to organizational performance objectives.

This book demystifies the process of calculating return on investment, examines how to use the formula, and explains how it is possible to use existing metrics to deliver a return on investment analysis and develop a commercial mindset by designing Learning and Development *for* Return on Investment.

Keywords

added value, audit, business case, design, evaluation, financial outcomes, learning and development, metrics, return on investment, strategic fit

Contents

Acknowledgments

I am grateful to Shyam Ramasubramony, who held my hand during the editorial process to make this a reality. A special thanks is also owed to Scott Isenberg and the team at Business Expert Press for giving me a platform to share my passion. My husband, Stephen, deserves a special mention for holding the fort and keeping the kids entertained whilst I try to write and keep polishing the halo. Finally, I would like to thank my former employer, Britvic Soft Drinks, for giving me the opportunity to work on a transformation project and my then manager, Gill Box, for turning my career on its head. That experience introduced me to the joys of organization and people development that added real value to the bottom line, leading me to where I am today.

List of Figures and Tables

CHAPTER 1

Introduction

In Learning and Development circles return on investment (ROI) is something that is quite often discussed in whispers in corridors, wide eyed, and with increasing amounts of anxiety. ROI involves formulas and some kind of financial analysis, and results in the learning practitioner developing the look of the condemned as they try to prove that something as intangible as changes in behavior, skills development, or knowledge can be measured and plotted on a graph. Recent research found "that just 35 percent of organizations measure the business results of any learning programs, and only 15 percent measure return on investment." (Ho, 2016)

The purpose of this book is to demystify the process of calculating ROI, explain how to use the formula, and enable learning practitioners to understand that it is possible to use existing mechanisms to deliver ROI analysis and develop a commercial mindset by designing learning and development *for* ROI.

Defining Evaluation

There is no single universally accepted definition of evaluation, and evaluation can mean many different things. Scriven (1991, 39) describes evaluation as "the process of determining the merit, worth or value of something or the product of that process." Whereas Russ-Eft (2014, 550) defines evaluation as "the systematic and on going processes for gathering data about programmes, organizations, and whole societies to enhance knowledge and decision making." Patton (2008, 38) explains that evaluation contributes to decision making as it allows those making decisions to make "judgments about the programme, improve or further develop programme effectiveness, inform decisions about future programming, and/or increase understanding." The common themes within literature regarding evaluation include the following:

- An assessment methodology that is systematic
- A focus on something that has intrinsic or extrinsic value to the person or organization
- A judgment that is delivered to provide a valuation of outcomes or impact on something
- A feature which is useful or advantageous

Return on Investment as an Evaluation Method

One of the reasons that ROI can seem so daunting is that it is difficult to ascertain the direct and indirect benefits that a development intervention can deliver. The level of learning that an individual takes from a development intervention is considered to be immeasurable in terms of before and after. They might demonstrate the development of knowledge by regurgitating facts, but learning, at least effective learning, should have a whole person impact, which is more difficult to quantify. It is certainly impossible to measure, for example, the financial impact of someone who is thinking or behaving differently, especially if that change is subtle and only noticeable over a period of time, or in a particular situation.

In approaching the concept of ROI, it is important to remember the common themes of evaluation. By systematically approaching ROI calculations from the perspective of outcomes that are valued by the organization and which demonstrate the usefulness or advantage that has occurred as a result of learning or development, it is possible to remove the indefinable and indistinguishable from the evaluation process.

The Importance of Return on Investment

The Holy Grail of ROI has been expounded by human resource (HR) professional bodies and literature for some years now, but as with all best practices it is important to consider the reason why being able to understand and calculate ROI is so critical not just as a learning practitioner, but for anyone working in human resource management (HRM).

Put simply someone, somewhere has provided resources, whether in time, people, or money, including the learning practitioners salary or fee and that someone, whether an institution, organization, or individual, will want to know what those resources have been used for. More importantly, they will want to know whether, having invested the resource, it has been worthwhile or whether they could or should have used that resource better elsewhere. Learning practitioners need to understand that investors and business leaders "expect every business activity to provide a financial or non financial 'return' for the money allocated." (Pangarkar and Kirkwood, 2013)

HR and learning and development have been considered a cost center in businesses for too long, and HR functions and leaders have been content with arguing their value based on non-financial returns such as employee performance improvements. In tough economic conditions or competitive markets, cost efficiency is a key lever of organizational performance, which is short hand for saying HR budgets will be cut and squeezed until there is nothing left. Cairns (2012) states that "business leaders will continue to challenge expenditures for training and development unless HR and learning practitioners can demonstrate the value in a way that goes beyond offering superficial metrics." The ROI of development interventions must therefore be communicated in terms of outcomes that are valued by the organization, which are business metrics and financial measures.

Overcoming the Fear of Numbers

The reason why a sizable proportion of learning practitioners avoid ROI, or at least resist having to use financial metrics, is because they are unfamiliar with the commercial aspects of business or are uncomfortable with numbers. Sometimes, the impression is given by learning practitioners that numbers are scary and should be avoided unless it is counting the number of participants who are attending a workshop. The only way to overcome a fear of numbers is by getting to know them and understanding that they are a tool, which releases the learning and development agenda and development activities from being considered to be a nice to have within the organization. A learning practitioner's best friend in the organization should be someone in the finance department, ideally a business analyst. Learning practitioners should schedule time to spend time with them, ask their advice, and learn from them. It will be the most important connection that can be made when trying to understand what outcomes are valued by the organization and how they are measured.

Summary

- There is no single universally accepted definition of evaluation.
- Systematically approach ROI calculations from the perspective of outcomes valued by the organization and demonstrate the usefulness of development interventions.
- Business leaders expect you to provide both financial and nonfinancial values added for resources invested.
- Communicate ROI in terms of business and financial outcomes that are valued by the organization.
- A key connection in the organization should be someone in the finance department, ideally a business analyst.

CHAPTER 2

The Growth of Strategic Learning and Development

The world is changing fast, and organizations are no longer content to allow functions to amble along without demonstrating that they are adding something to the strategic direction of the organization. The learning and development function must provide a strategic response to match the learning and development activities with the organizational environment. Taking into account the full scope of the function's activities, the learning practitioner must ensure that the structure of the function, its practices, and procedures contribute to the achievement of the organization's goals. Strategic management is a discipline, which focuses on the long-term continuity of the organization. This requires an assessment of how resources can be allocated to ensure that learning and development activities are used to take advantage of opportunities available to the organization and respond to issues or challenges that the organization faces.

The strategic management of the learning and development function is concerned with contributing to sustainable performance within the organization and setting strategies and plans based on the analysis of external and internal factors. There are a number of forces within the business environment, which are causing business leaders to turn their attention to the people resource:

- Key skills shortages
- Requirement for a more flexible and adaptable workforce
- Difficulty in aligning individual employees to organizational goals
- The cost of high levels of staff turnover

- Low productivity
- Health and safety issues, legal consequences, and risk of fines
- Speed of technology change
- Globalization
- Social changes and the evolving meaning of work

The strategic management of learning and development involves more than simply responding to the business strategy, but also involves shaping the evolving business strategy. This approach to learning and development deviates from the traditional focus on training administration and reactive delivery of instruction toward an entity, which is focused on developing a strong learning culture, adopts a strategic approach to learning and development, and focuses on organizational change and sustainable business performance.

The Importance of Learning and Development

It wouldn't be possible to write a book about designing learning and development for return on investment if there wasn't an underlying belief that learning and development can and does add value to the strategic goals of the organization. There is also another principle that must be considered, that is, that learning and development is a fundamental component to the achievement of strategic goals. This goes beyond learning and development being a nice to have, instead it is a belief, which advocates that the best learning and development functions are essential to the creation and achievement of the strategic goals of the organization.

If learning and development is to have a positive impact on organizational performance outcomes then the learning and development strategy must encompass short-term operational tactics, medium-term plans, and long-term strategic programs. This involves the learning practitioner developing an insight into the current organizational people resource requirements in regards to knowledge, skills, and abilities to build the organization's capacity and achieve today's goals as well as proactively developing the people resource capabilities requisite for the future people resource needs of the organization.

Therefore, the strategic management of learning and development goes beyond simply delivering skills development and instead advances and shapes the human resource to continuously adapt in response to the organizational environment. Key questions that the learning and development function must answer include the following:

- What is known about the environmental context of the organization and how does that impact the learning and development strategy?
- What role should learning and development play in shaping and achieving the strategic goals of the organization?
- How is alignment achieved between the learning and development strategy and the organizational strategic goals?
- What skills, knowledge, and abilities does the organization need now, and in the future?
- How is learning and development capability being developed to meet the needs within the organization?
- How will a pipeline of talent be successfully developed, grown, and nurtured within the organization?
- How will learning and development interventions continuously improve and be evaluated?

Who Should Organizations Invest In?

The budget allocated to learning and development is normally finite, and as such the usual approach to learning and development budgets is to make difficult decisions in regards to which sections of the employee population should be invested in. When the economic climate gets tough, the finance department proposes two areas for cost saving and reduction: the marketing budget and learning and development budget. Although organizational resources are limited, a strategic management approach to learning and development turns the budget question on its head. Instead of waiting for the business to throw coppers into the budget begging bowl, learning and development builds its strategy and explains, using a business case (see Chapter 6), what budget is required in order to support the organizational strategy as effectively as possible. This approach avoids the unsolvable dilemma often faced by learning and development as to whom the organization should invest in. Investment should be made into areas of the business that add value and helps achieve the organization's strategic goals. Strategic management shifts the focus away from competing demands to direct learning and development activity and organizational budget allocation to those initiatives that support the development of the human resource as a whole. Although some human resources may be more important to the delivery of the strategic goals than others, it is important that learning and development concentrate their efforts on ensuring the human resource capability as a whole is developed in line with the organization's strategic agenda. Only the full utilization of the organization's most important asset, its people, will ensure that the organization achieves competitive advantage. Like any other asset within the business, under investment can have devastating consequences in the long term.

Garavan's Model (2007)

Garavan (2007) proposed a multilevel model of strategic human resource development (HRD), which operates within four levels of dynamic context:

- **Context:** The interaction between learning and development and the global environment in which the organization operates. Taking into account local influences (political, economic, and industry trends), national factors (social factors, labor market trends, and national culture), and multinational circumstances (technological changes, international law, and regulation).
- **Internal Context:** The internal context in which the learning practitioner operates, encompassing strategy, organizational design, culture, and leadership style.
- **Job Value and Uniqueness:** The perception of the strategic importance attached to a particular job and how learning and development should be applied in each circumstance.
- **Professional Expectations:** Individual expectations of the learning practitioner in regards to how their potential will be used, their employability as a result of professional development, and their career ambitions.

Garavan (2007) argued that the learning practitioner should operate an open-systems approach to the strategic management of learning and development within the organization in order to enable it to develop an environment where strategic goals and sustainable performance can be achieved. In order for this ambition to be realized, learning practitioners must develop a strategy, which is vertically aligned to the business strategic and horizontally aligned to other human resource strategic practices.

The Peterson Model

Peterson (2008) model of HRD is founded upon system-thinking ideas. Peterson (2008) while acknowledging the external environment focuses primarily upon the internal environment includes the capacity of the learning and development function to develop strategic goals and the ability of the learning practitioner to perform the role of a strategic partner. The Peterson model assumes that political, economic, social, legal, and cultural forces influence strategic learning and development. Three dimensions influence whether the organizational response to these forces will be proactive or reactive:

- A culture of learning,
- A commitment to performance improvement, and
- A capacity for strategic engagement.

Peterson (2008) suggests that the learning and development function is responsible for strategic leadership in regards to developing the human capital within the organization. The onus is on the learning practitioner to implement exceptional initiatives, which create value for the organization and evaluate their actions to ensure they deliver development that increases the knowledge, skills, abilities, motivation, and empowerment of the employee population in order to deliver the organizational mission.

Developing Strategic Fit

Strategic management of learning and development therefore relies on the learning and development function, ensuring that resources are employed to support organization's strategic goals and are responsive to the environmental opportunities and threats. Every part of the learning and development strategy should be mutually supportive of other HR strategy initiatives, the functional strategies of other business units, and the organizational as a whole. However, this process is not a linear process resulting in a fixed plan instead strategic management requires the approach to learning and development to be adaptive and evolve in response to the changing organizational strategy while staying flexible enough to respond to environmental forces. The learning practitioner must develop as a strategic partner of the organization, giving time to understanding how the organization operates, identifying issues that are causing managers and employees pain, and establishing opportunities for improvement to support progress toward the achievement of the organization's strategic goal. This requires the learning practitioner to become comfortable with the commercial aspects of the organization and be business-focused in addressing the development of the organization's people resource.

The most important element of strategic management is the focus on ensuring that learning and development resources are utilized to deliver the maximum value to organizational performance and create culture of learning through learning and development processes including the following:

- Organizational development
- Performance management
- Skills and knowledge development
- Secondments and project work
- Peer-to-peer learning
- Coaching and mentoring
- Talent management
- Succession planning
- Career development

With the focus on strategic management, the learning practitioner must not lose sight of delivering high levels of performance internally and ensuring that learning and development systems and processes are well developed to ensure that analysis, learning management, evaluation, reporting, performance management, productivity, and record keeping all deliver a high standard of service to internal clients.

Theories Underpinning Learning and Development

Learning and development can make a significant contribution to organizational success, by integrating learning and development with the organizational strategy and adapting the learning and development strategy to respond to the individual, team, functional, and organizational development needs. There are two approaches to learning and development strategy, which can be adopted.

- Best fit
- Best practice

Best-fit Learning and Development

The contingency approach to learning and development is focused on strategic integration between the learning and development strategy and the organizational strategy. The model contends that learning and development practices and policies will be most productive when they are compatible with the organizational strategy. The contingency model is therefore focused upon the interaction between learning and development and organizational strategy to optimize organizational performance. In this respect, there is no best way to approach learning and development, rather there is only the best fit for the organization in which the learning practitioner is operating.

Best-fit strategy development focuses on adopting interventions, which fits best with the external business environmental context and the internal fit with HR policies and practices. The best-fit approach was developed by Schuler and Jackson (1987), who identified the connection between competitive advantage, employee performance, and HR practices. The best-fit approach has been criticized for not acknowledging the presence of employee issues and ignoring the pressure from operations management on strategic practice resulting in incoherence between the operational delivery of learning and development and the strategic direction.

Best-practice Learning and Development

A second approach to learning and development strategy is the Universalist best-practice approach introduced by Guest (1997) who suggested that there was an ideal set of practices, which would deliver improved productivity and effectiveness. Although identified as delivering superior economic performance, employee well-being and employee relations, there are few organizations where which have the majority of the high commitment management practice recommended by Guest (1997) in place. From a learning and development perspective there are number of best practices, which can be adopted such as:

- Personalized learning focused on the individual learner
- Self-service and self-directed learning and development
- E-learning and mobile learning
- Integrating learning into work processes
- Content curation
- Knowledge management
- Coaching by line managers and peers
- On-the-job training
- Blended learning
- Facilitated team and group learning

However, there is little agreement between academics and practitioners as to what set of practices need to be applied to achieve the desired outcome. Therefore, universal learning and development best practice remains a theoretical concept.

Summary

- Strategic management is a discipline, which focuses on the long-term continuity of the organization.
- The strategic management of learning and development involves more than simply responding to the business strategy, but is also involved in shaping the evolving business strategy.

- The strategic management of learning and development advances and shapes the human resource to continuously adapt in response to the organizational environment.
- Direct learning and development activity and organizational budget allocation to those initiatives that support the development of the human resource as a whole.
- Learning practitioners must develop a strategy, which is vertically aligned to the business strategy and horizontally aligned to other human resource strategic practices.
- From a learning and development perspective there are number of best practices, which can be adopted to deliver improved productivity and effectiveness.

CHAPTER 3

The Learning and Development Cycle

The most common model of the training cycle is usually presented as a four-step model:

1. Training needs analysis
2. Design
3. Deliver
4. Evaluate

However, the learning and development cycle (LDC) is more holistic and systematic and takes into account the key themes of evaluation discussed in Chapter 1. It encompasses the alignment of the learning and development strategy to the business strategy as an essential element.

When designing for return on investment (ROI), it is essential that each stage of the LDC is approached within the context of what outcomes are most valued by the organization. By keeping organizational outcomes front of mind in the design process, you will make sure that whatever is delivered whether in diagnosis, design, implementation, or evaluation, it will always be aligned to the criteria defined as the most important to the organization.

Evaluation—Begin with the End in Mind

This stage of the cycle will be explored in detail in Chapter 4. As shown in Figure 3.1, Evaluation is at the beginning and the end of the LDC. This reflects a sentiment expressed by Stephen Covey (2004, 98) who argued that "to begin with the end in mind means to start with a clear

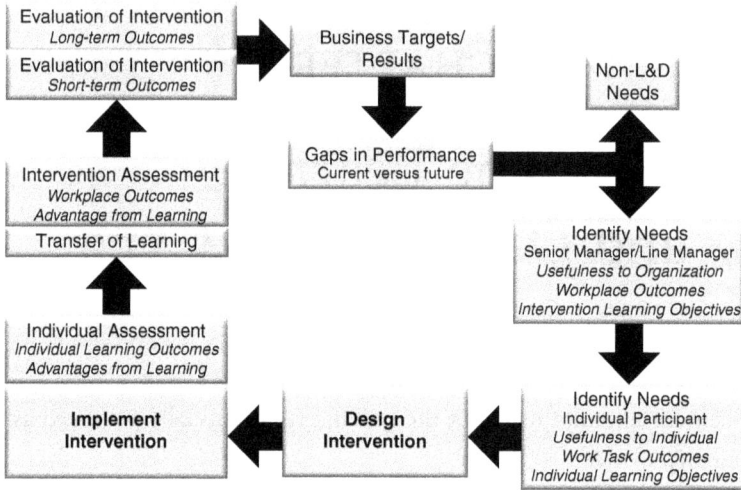

Figure 3.1 Learning and development cycle

understanding of your destination." It requires that the learning practitioner understands what interventions have been delivered historically and what affect these interventions have had in terms of organizational outcomes.

A key piece of research at the start of the LDC is to develop an understanding of what performance outcomes the organization must deliver in order to achieve its strategic objectives and an analysis of performance gaps between the current state and the desired future state. Whereas "senior leaders live in the 'input' and 'output' world" (Cheung-Judge and Holbeche, 2015, 120), it is the responsibility of the learning practitioner to provide a strategic evaluation which focuses on the system throughput needed in regards to culture, capability, capacity, and skills in order for the organization to achieve its key strategic priorities. It is at this point that a ROI target can be calculated.

At the end of the LDC, the evaluation provides a review of what has happened and whether the intervention(s) achieved the strategic objectives set at the beginning of the LDC and moved the organization forward toward its desired strategic goal. It also determines whether outcomes valued by the organization have been realized and how useful the intervention or interventions have been in terms of providing a learning advantage which can be applied back in the workplace by individuals, groups, and the organization as whole. It is at this point that a ROI result can be reported. Furthermore, the performance of the learning and development function itself can be audited.

Identifying Learning and Development Needs

This stage of the cycle will be explored in more detail in Chapter 5. Identifying needs requires the learning practitioner to work backward to understand the workplace outcomes and learning objectives that will fit the organization, team, and individual needs. In this stage, analysis techniques are used to determine what development needs exist within the organization, which will result in closing the performance gaps identified during the evaluation phase.

Designing the Intervention

The design stage of the LDC will be explored in more detail in Chapter 7. The emphasis in designing learning and development for ROI is not on the content of the intervention but on the process of learning that is being used during the intervention. It takes into account the environmental influences, the interconnectedness and interdependencies between parts of the organization, groups, and individual employees, and how the system operates in order to determine what must be done to deliver sustainable organizational effectiveness.

Implementing the Intervention

The implementation stage will be explored in more detail in Chapter 8. It is during this stage that the appropriateness of the intervention in regards of delivering the intended organizational priorities is fully realized. The implementation stage also includes a form of assessment of learning, which evaluates whether the planned performance gaps have been addressed. The implementation stage is therefore the beginning of the process of the end of cycle evaluation in regards to the usefulness or learning advantage that the intervention has delivered to the individual participants.

Organizational Attitudes to Learning and Development

At this stage, it is worth examining the impact that organizational attitudes to learning and development can have on the successful implementation of the LDC. Without doubt many organizational leaders will verbally support the notion that employee development is important to the achievement of the business strategy. However, in practice many managers and leaders behave very differently when it comes to providing financial resources for learning and development activities or allowing adequate time for employee development. Despite huge investments in business and process reengineering, few organizations invest a proportionate amount of resource in the people development that is required to make the change successful. An understanding of what factors impact the attitude of organizational leaders toward learning and development must be acknowledged. Unless the learning practitioner is lucky enough to work for an enlightened organizational leader, organizational attitudes to learning and development are influenced by:

- **Internal Factors.** Crisis, skills gaps which directly impact on operations, or difficulties in recruiting to strategically important positions.
- **External Factors.** Losing competitive advantage, changing technology, which directly impact on operations, political forces, or legislative changes, or a tightening of the labor market leading to a shortage of key skills available.
- **Circumstantial Differences.** The changing nature of an industry, employee profiles, and the size or type of challenges or opportunities faced by the organization.
- **Benefits.** The perception of benefits that learning and development delivers.
- **Costs.** The cost of learning and development versus the perceived benefits.

Bemoaning this situation is to ignore the responsibility that learning practitioners have in failing to deliver clarity regarding the ROI for development interventions. The sooner ROI is used by learning practitioners as part of their day to day activity, the sooner attitudes to learning and development will change. Challenging attitudes toward learning and development will be examined in Chapter 10.

Summary

- The LDC is more holistic, systemic, and takes into account the outcomes, which are valued by the organization at every stage.
- Evaluation is at the beginning and the end of the LDC.
- Strategic evaluation focuses on the system throughput needed in regards to culture, capability, capacity, and skills.
- Analysis techniques are used to identify development needs which, if addressed, will result in closing organization's performance gaps.
- The emphasis of designing learning and development *for* ROI is on the process of learning that is being used during the intervention.
- The factors that impact the attitude of organizational leaders toward learning and development are internal factors, external factors, circumstantial differences, costs, and benefits.

CHAPTER 4

The Evaluation Phase

If the most critical step in the learning and development cycle (LDC) is to build alignment to business strategy, then it makes sense to ensure that the learning practitioner has a clear idea of what the organization will look like the business strategy has been achieved. There are many models available to help understand the importance of describing goals fully, whether that is a Big Hairy Audacious Goal (Collins, 2001) or a Wildly Important Goal (Covey, 2015), but what is important is that both the learning practitioner and the rest of the organization are clear on:

- What does the organization look like?
- What does the organization feel like?
- How would our people behave toward each other, customers, suppliers, and so on?
- What would our competitors, suppliers, and customers say about us?
- How would employees talk about the organization?
- How would the managers behave toward their line reports?
- What skills, knowledge, and capability would exist in the organization?

Until the learning practitioner has a clear mental image of what the strategic goal for the organization is, it is difficult to diagnose the performance gap between where the organization is now (current state) and where the organization will be if organizational goals are achieved (future state).

A strategic goal can be likened to a holiday destination. There are many variations and possible holiday destinations that can be visited, depending on whether the traveler is looking for heat, snow, family friendly, adventure, city break, and so on. What clothes are packed into the suitcase and travel plans will be determined by your destination. A swimsuit is great if you are going to Miami Beach but perhaps not suitable for sightseeing in the Middle East or climbing Everest. Similarly, organizations can develop strategic goals, which are as different as a sun lounger is from a white water raft. Organizations may develop strategic goals that rely on, for example; high quality service, low price good, focused markets, differentiated ranges, global reach, local delivery, for profit, not-for-profit, and so on. Therefore; it is essential that before consideration is given to how to measure success, there is clarity on how to recognize success when it is achieved.

Begin with the End in Mind

Once there is clarity as to the strategic destination of the organization, the learning practitioner can begin working on some expectations in regards to what the organizational achievements may need to be in regards to required performance levels, in order for the organization to reach its strategic goals. Quite simply, this is identifying what measures, if achieved, will result in achieving the goal. Some measurements will track whether the strategic plan is on track, output measures. Other metrics will measure high impact activities that have a direct influence on the achievement of outcome, input measures. For example, if turnover is reduced, recruitment costs will fall.

It is important at this point to be clear that this does not require a reinvention of the organizational metric wheel. The best place to start when considering what the end will look like is to look at the performance measures that the organization has set itself. This ensures that the performance measures that are being used for evaluation are measuring outcomes, which are valued by the organization. There will most certainly be headline figures in regards to growth rates, revenue, and profit but within the business strategy will be the building blocks of the strategy presented as a clearly defined set of financial measures. If the organization has a robust business strategy, it will also include a detailed workforce plan. This should hopefully include information regarding a variety of people performance metrics expressed as a monetary value (Figure 4.1).

Example of People Metrics	Example of Performance Metrics
Employee population and headcount costs	Return on capital employed/employee utilization
Recruitment levels and costs	Revenue/Profitability per employee
Absence levels	Lost time accident rate
Employee satisfaction	Customer brand recognition/feedback levels
Redundancy and outplacement costs	Customer complaints/satisfaction rates/ response times
Learning and development costs	Time to market, e.g., new product development
Performance ratings	Sales, revenue, profit, profit margin, marginal cost
Competency, skills, and capability levels	Production efficiency
Workforce efficiency	Process effectiveness

Figure 4.1 People performance metrics examples

If no workforce plan exists, then it is essential that the learning practitioner works alongside the wider HR team and their colleagues in the finance department to ensure that a clear workforce plan is developed before diagnosing needs. Key questions that will need answering in order to define the end are as follows:

- What is the size and shape of the employee population?
- What new skills, knowledge, or abilities are required for the organization to achieve its desired future state?
- What existing skills, knowledge, or abilities need to be updated or will become redundant?
- What are the challenges and opportunities that the organization will face and in what way can learning and development contribute to overcoming performance hurdles?
- What changes need to occur in organizational behavior and culture for the future state to be achieved?
- What knowledge needs to arise in the organization, and where and when does that knowledge need to be available?
- What do we know we don't know at this point, and what impact does that have on the strategic plans?
- What are the risks directly related to learning and development and where do we need to develop contingency plans?

Measuring the Impact of Learning and Development

All employee performance improvements whether in knowledge, skills, abilities, or behavior will lead directly or indirectly to greater organizational effectiveness resulting in increased profitability or improved efficiency leading to reduced costs. This is a bold claim, and often it is hard to identify the effect of subtle changes in individuals. However, just like it is not possible to spot the incremental physical growth and changing maturity of a child on a day-to-day basis, performance changes are gradual and a sum of the system.

From a LDC perspective, once the people performance metrics, which measure the success of the business strategy, have been identified, it is then possible to begin developing a set of learning and development performance measures. This will be both return on expectation (ROE), which measures success in terms of organizational environment, behaviors, culture, knowledge, and skills and metrics that can be used to determine the monetary, or return on investment (ROI), people performance improvements. Since these measures already exist in the organization, it is also possible to use existing reporting mechanisms in order to track the identified metrics on a regular basis. It is recommended that the learning practitioner requests a regular report from a friendly business analyst in the finance department at this stage.

Typologies of Evaluation

There are numerous types of evaluation that learning practitioners can engage in, all of which have a different purpose, time frame, and usefulness in the evaluation process as shown in Figure 4.2.

The choice of evaluation type will depend on what information is required by key stakeholders within the organization to make decisions in regards to the added value that the learning and development function is delivering to the organization. The type of evaluation will also be reliant on the skills and knowledge of the learning practitioner in conducing evaluations, as well as the time resource available for this type of activity. The decisions made about the type, quantity, and quality of evaluation used is determined by organizational needs. However, in regards

Figure 4.2 Typologies of evaluation

Type of Evaluation	What Is It?	When to Use	Best Use
Ex-Ante	An evaluation of current state and performance gaps to develop forecasts for what might happen as a result of the intervention	Evaluation stage start of cycle	When developing the business case for program and intervention proposals, to determine strategic fit and whether the benefits of the program will outweigh the risks/costs
Formative	Assessment when designing to develop and improvement intervention	Identify needs stage	When introducing a new intervention or following a pilot of the intervention
Summative	An end of intervention assessment, both of individual learner and intervention	Evaluation stage end of cycle	To report on the ROI and ROE of the intervention, program, and learning and development strategy outcomes
Comprehensive	Interactive evaluation process addressing questions relating to intervention viability and improvement	Evaluation stage start of cycle and identify needs stage	Determines the program effectiveness (did it deliver what you set out to deliver)
Outcomes	Evaluation of short-term and long-term organizational behavior changes that have occurred as a result of a program or intervention	Evaluation stage	To examine the short- and long-term changes in behavior delivered by the LDC
Theory driven	Evaluation which examines how and why the intervention worked, or did not work	Evaluation stage	Providing stakeholders with information useful in improving existing or future programs and interventions
Impact	A longitudinal comparison study of the long-term changes resulting from an intervention or program	Evaluation stage	To influence policy and understand organizational performance outcomes that can be attributed to the LDC
Metaevaluation	Formal evaluation of all the evaluation system, including evaluation planning, processes, management, and usefulness	Evaluation stage	Provides key stakeholders in evaluation information with an evaluation of the usefulness of the evaluation system in guiding the planning and management of interventions and programs

to winning the battle of hearts and minds to the cause of learning and development, how much the learning practitioner values the usefulness of evaluation will determine the robustness of the evaluation that takes place.

Summary

- The learning practitioner needs to ensure they have a clear idea of what the organization will look like when it achieves the business strategy.
- Begin with the End in Mind means establishing performance expectations of organizational achievements by identifying what measures, if achieved, will result in achieving the strategic goal.
- If no workforce plan exists, then it is essential that a plan is developed before diagnosing needs.
- The best place to start is to look at the performance measures that the organization uses in the business strategy.
- By using performance measures that already exist in the organization, it is also possible to use existing reporting mechanisms in order to track the identified metrics on a regular basis.
- There are numerous types of evaluation all of which have a different purpose, time frame, and usefulness in the evaluation process.
- The type, quantity, and quality of evaluation used will be determined by organizational needs.

CHAPTER 5

Development Needs Analysis

When identifying needs it is important to revisit the common themes of evaluation. In Chapter 1 it was explained that return on investment (ROI) calculations should be systematically approached from the perspective of outcomes that are valued by the organization and which demonstrate the usefulness or advantage that has occurred as a result of learning or development. Development needs analysis (DNA) must be a systematic approach. The learning practitioner must use a systematic process to identify needs, but must also approach the analysis from the perspective of the organization being a system, where the different parts of the organization are interdependent upon each other. Within the learning and development cycle (LDC), the learning practitioner is responsible for developing knowledge and understanding about how the system operates and the relationship between the different parts of the organization. This approach also means that development interventions should not be developed in isolation but with an overview of the interrelationship between each element of the learning and development strategy.

Systems Theory

This approach to DNA relies on an understanding of systems theory, which was first introduced by Von Bertalanffy (1950). In developing an outline of general systems theory, Von Bertalanffy (1950, 142) summarizes "a scientific doctrine of 'wholeness,'" and explains that the complexity found in all systems, including those found in organizations, demonstrates the existence of interactions and interdependencies that work together to provide stability within the system. This balance is maintained despite the exchange of energy and materials between the internal and external systems.

Most organizational problems or opportunities are considered in the form of a simple cause-and-effect model based on what can be ascertained by close proximity between inputs and outputs. Thus, generation of solutions will be based on short-term fixes, which produce improvements quickly. However, from a systems perspective such as simple approach ignores the complex forces, which exist within an organization, which often results in short-term fixes resulting in significant long-term costs. For example, cost cutting to improve profits in the short term can lead to a lack of essential investment resulting in long-term business decline. Therefore, an appreciation of an organization's system causes attention to be paid to long-term consequences of actions taken to ensure the desired outcomes are achieved and the long-term health of the organization is maintained.

Systems theory challenges the learning practitioner to look beyond the immediate presenting symptoms that are identified and require fixing within the organization. Instead, the learning practitioner should approach a development need by thinking about the organizational system as a whole, causes the development practitioner to consider what needs to happen from a people perspective to create a better product, improved service, cost efficiency, improved employee engagement, or increased capacity.

One challenge of course is not getting so tied up in the system that it becomes impossible to take any action. Systems are complex and from a systems dynamics perspective there is no end to the system. There is always one more aspect or context to consider. Analysis paralysis is not the desired result for a systems approach, but examining the causes of the symptoms is an essential part of learning and development design, which requires the learning practitioner to adopt a comprehensive approach to problem identification. When undertaken in this way, a systems approach is a simple commonsense thinking approach, avoiding sticking plaster solutions and delivering results that really make a difference.

The Learning Organization

Systems theory was used by Peter Senge (1990, 3) as the foundation of the concept of the learning organization which seeks to make sense of the interrelationship between different parts of the system to enable the people resource in the organization to "continually expand their capacity to create the results they truly desire, where new and expansive patterns of thinking are nurtured, where collective aspiration is set free, and where people are continually learning to see the whole together." The premise for the learning organization was the idea that only organizations that could utilize people's capacity and commitment to learn could develop the flexibility and adaptability to respond to change.

Senge (1990) identified five disciplines converge to establish a learning organization. They are as follows:

- Systems thinking
- Personal mastery
- Mental models
- Building shared vision
- Team learning

The learning and development function supports the development of the learning organization by providing the structure, guiding ideas, tools and opportunities for people to make sense of the situations they face. In addition learning and development can create the space for people to engage in reflection, and encourage the freedom to develop their learning capacity.

The Vanguard Method

Seddon and Brand (2008) developed The Vanguard Method as a systems checking, outside in, customer approach to change management. They proposed that taking a customer view, rather than an organizational view, would enable managers to understand where inefficiency exists and develop plans for improvement. The Vanguard Model offers three steps to performance improvement:

- **Check:** Asking What and Why of current performance within the organizational system
- **Plan:** Planning what levers to use within the system, which will result in change
- **Do:** Taking direct action

Learning practitioners can adopt The Vanguard Method to implement systems theory in practice and develop confidence in planning and executing learning interventions that is based on knowledge of the organizational system.

The Systematic Approach to Learning and Development

Arnold and Silvester (2005) offered a systematic approach to learning and development to ensure that activities are based upon a diagnostic analysis of development needs, the design meets the specific requirements of the organization, and the intervention is evaluated for success. These three levels are described as:

- **Assessment of Needs:** Organization, task, and job analysis
- **Design and Delivery:** Definition of a clear aim and objectives, the development of learning methods, selection of participants, and intervention delivery
- **Transfer and Evaluation:** Supporting the transfer of learning and evaluating learning at individual, team, and organizational level

Each level of interaction is interdependent, forming a self-supporting tripod that delivers effective learning and development. For learning and development to deliver benefit, each level must be present as missing or poorly formed levels will result in failure.

Model of Organizational Balance

The model of Organizational Balance (Figure 5.1) provides a map to navigate specific elements of organizational performance from the perspective of a people-centered ecosystem. It identifies the human processes and interrelationships and different interactions that impact upon organizational performance. Every element of the ecosystem is both part of, a determinate of, and a product of the system, and

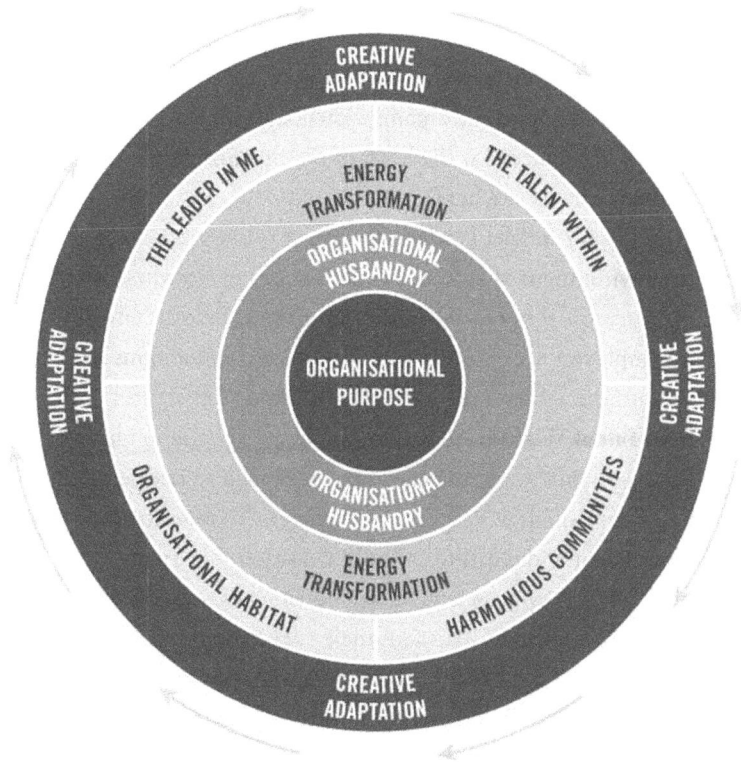

Figure 5.1 Model of organizational balance

can only be sustained if kept in balance with the other organizational elements. When introducing development interventions, the learning practitioner needs to be aware that by changing any one part of an organization results in a shift in the balance of the organization's ecosystem—for good or bad.

From a humanism perspective, it could be argued that the continued success or eventual failure of organizational endeavors will be determined by how much the organization works with, rather than against, human nature and the organization's ecosystem. If development interventions work against the organization's human ecosystem, then resistance, drag, and natural barriers will affect performance. However, by working within the organization's system, performance will become self-sustaining.

Elements of Organizational Balance

- **Organizational Purpose:** The reason an organization exists, giving meaning to the organization's day-to-day activities. The center of balance is at the heart of the organization and must explain why we are here.

- **The Leader in Me:** Leaders contribute to the creation of an environment of sustainable performance; regardless of culture, it is through the leadership process that the efforts of employees are co-ordinated, given direction, and moved toward the achievement of the organization's purpose.

- **The Talent Within:** All employees in an organization have talent in something, but they may need help to release their talent potential by supporting employees in understanding their talent and creating an individual's job role around the talents they possess. The individual has a responsibility to develop a self-awareness of their talent and develop their capacity to use it. Leaders must support employees to align their individual purpose with the achievement of organizational purpose.

- **Harmonious Communities:** Leaders and employees must work together to create an environment, which facilitates individuals, teams, and functions in building relationships and enable cooperation and collaboration in order to collectively help the organization pursue its purpose and strategy. By tapping into the networked organization, it is possible to expand the talent pool from pockets of outstanding performance to a successful sharing of expertise, knowledge, skill, and experience.

- **Organizational Habitat:** Organizational balance can only be achieved if the structure and design of an organization is capable of coping with changes in the internal and external environment while still providing stability to manage the organizational activities.

- **Organizational Husbandry:** An organization needs to promote sustainable organizational processes and practices through the development of a methodology and methods of approaching the organizational resources sensitively.

- **Creative Adaptation:** Developing the creative capability to continually innovate organizational operations to shift toward favorable and sustainable performance as the result of changes taking place in the external environment and more importantly, being able to proactively manage changes rather than react to changes thrust upon the organization.

- **Energy Transformation:** It is essential to analyze and evaluate the effectiveness of activities taking place to ensure they are having the impact they should be having, and that the time and resource (energy) committed are delivering added value and transforming the performance within the organization. Energy transformation enables an organization to answer the question: Is what we are doing having the impact we want it to and more importantly, is it aligned to our core purpose?

- **Organizational Cycling:** The environment in which an organization operates will affect the way in which the organization carries out its operations, for example, the development of new technology, societal and cultural shifts, and regulatory changes. These influences on organizational balance combined with those forces, which can cause disruption, affect the ability of an organization to create the environment for sustainable performance.

It is possible for organization to achieve its strategic goals without balance in its system, but it cannot perform to its full potential; the organizational environment is often chaotic and performance levels will not be sustainable over the long term. Any ecosystem changes can occur both inside and outside the control of the organization therefore the organizational system will need to adjust to accomodate these change in order to remain in balance. The key to continued peak performance is to identify the development needs required to maintain balance within the organization.

Identifying Needs

The learning practitioner needs to take a holistic and systematic perspective toward identifying development needs. The key question is "what evidence is needed to identify needs?" The truth is, there is a myriad of data sources available, and for the analysis to demonstrate areas where usefulness or advantage can be achieved. It is recommended that several sources be used from those available (Figure 5.2).

Figure 5.2 Data types

Data Type	Definition	Examples
Hard	Quantitative aspects based on measured facts and figures	• Annual report and trading figures • Financial reports • Business strategies • Channel strategies • Absence rates • Turnover rates • Headcount • Diversity figures • Grievances • Terminations
Soft	Qualitative aspects based on abstract information	• Employee opinion survey • Customer feedback • Market research data • Brand value/Identity • Cultural health check • 360-degree review
Vitality	The vigor, energy, and enthusiasm of people within or using the organization	• Exit interviews • Employee engagement survey • Voice of the customer survey • Employee pulse survey • Customer insight • Vitality index • Channel strategies
Proficiency	Capability, competence, skill, and expertise of the people within the organization	• Pre-employment screening • Productivity measures • Retention statistics • Return on time invested (ROTI) index • Performance management/appraisal database • Benchmarking • Competence acquisition • Continuous improvement • Capability audit • Substitute to star ratio • Skills database

Figure 5.2 Data types (Continued)

Data Type	Definition	Examples
Power	Political strength, personal power, or hierarchical authority of groups and individuals within the organizational system	• Stakeholder mapping • Organizational reporting structure • Informal hierarchy—organizational gatekeepers • Dotted line reporting matrix • Flow of information
Market	Competitors and industry within which the organization operates	• Government statistics • Competitor data • Customer insight data • Industry data • Market research
Stakeholder	Individuals and groups who have a vested interest in the organization	• Shareholder reports • Customer satisfaction survey • Supplier feedback survey • Regulator reports
Practice	Occupation or profession-specific information	• Occupational body reports and surveys • Professional body reports an d surveys

Dialogic Data Collection Methods

Social construction theory was emerged from the field of sociology shortly before World War II. It explores the philosophical question around reality and knowledge in an attempt to explain what is real from a sociological perspective. Berger and Luckmann (1966, 54) explain that "language bridges different zones within the reality of everyday life and integrates them into a meaningful whole." What this means is that the individual's understanding of the organization is not real in the sense of a solid object like a table. Instead, organizational reality is a result of the way employees interact and talk about the reality of an organization. It is a social construct. An organization, therefore, is not real but represents the ideas, conventions, and beliefs discussed by the organizational players. Understanding social construction theory arms the learning practitioner with a tool to gather organizational data through methods, which utilize dialogue. Dialogic data collection methods focus on language and meaning making through interaction and discussion (Figure 5.3). Additionally, dialogic data collection methods can be used to move the organization forward through diagnostic development interventions which change

Figure 5.3 Dialogic data collection methods

Collection Method	Methodology
Observation	Observing people in their role, team, and group interaction. Spending time with organizational players to observe behavior across functions and during the performance of specific tasks or activities.
Interviews	Structured, semistructured, or unstructured one to one interviews with individuals in roles or functions of investigation.
Focus groups	Single function or mixed function focus groups assembled to participate in discussion about a key learning and development theme.
Performance inquiry	Actors perform various organizational scenarios which organizational players are asked to discuss in regards to their applicability to their reality of the organization.
Storytelling	Individual employees share stories to reveal their reality of working within the organization on key research themes.
Whole system	High involvement systemic approaches to development engaging individuals, groups, and functions who are directly affected by the development theme being investigated. Examples include Open Space Technology and World Cafe.
Field visits	Group visits to key external stakeholders such as customers or suppliers, incorporating direct observation, interviews, or focus groups to gather information from the operating environment.

the way employees talk about the organization, and therefore create a new organizational reality. Dialogic data collection methods provide soft, vitality, proficiency, and power data. This data can be analyzed using qualitative data analysis techniques such as content, discourse or conversation analysis, and so on.

Diagnostic Data Collection Methods

Diagnostic data is based on facts that can be analyzed. Diagnostic data collection methods predominately use information found in reports, documents, and through database providing hard, stakeholder, proficiency, and market data (Figure 5.4). This data can be analyzed using quantitative data analysis techniques and statistical analysis.

Figure 5.4 Diagnostic data collection methods

Collection Method	Methodology
Documentation	Existing documents such as annual reports, regulatory audits, financial information, consumer satisfaction reports, performance reports, and so on
Online information	Information on the intranet or intranet relating to the operating environment, the organization as whole of different parts of the organization
Questionnaires	A survey using online or printed questions with a choice of answers designed for the purpose of statistical analysis
Storyboarding	A sequence of drawings or diagrams to depict interactions or processes within the organization to share insights regarding input and output flows within the organization.
Graffiti board	Providing a physical or virtual space, such as a whiteboard or online message board, for people to record comments or reactions to relevant topics or themes.
Culture mapping	A tool for tangible, observable behavior-based analysis surveying specific levers identifying the building blocks of an organization's cultural DNA.

The Diagnostic Team

The learning and development function can very often been viewed as an isolated department that only interacts with the organization when it is delivering a training course or a coaching session. However, when approaching DNA from a systemic perspective, who does the DNA because a wider question that simply the learning practitioner. Although the learning practitioner may begin the DNA journey working on intuition or on the basis of a small amount of data, the DNA process will provide clarity about who else, from a diagnostic perspective, is needed to move the organization forward.

To collect and analyze the data, the learning practitioner needs to consider the following:

- Who should participate in collecting data?
- Who should be included in the sample population?
- Who should attend DNA interventions to have a positive influence on the dialogue?

- Who needs to have responsibility for and ownership of the data collected?
- Who should be part of the data analysis team?
- What feedback of the results from the data analysis is required, when and to whom?
- Who has the political capital/authority to be a key sponsor of the identified development programs/intervention?

Creating Advantage from DNA

The DNA process can be useful in more ways than simply delivering results from data feedback to feed into the design process. DNA interventions can in themselves support the organization in moving forward and help to achieve valued organizational outcomes. By proactively engaging employees in DNA activities and by providing them with personal development and an opportunity to influence the LDC, it is possible to reward and support the employees in pursuing organizational priorities. The use of dialogic DNA interventions and presentation of the results of the data analysis can provide a powerful shift in the way employees discuss the organization and thus, the social construction of the organization. This can result in positive improvements in organizational performance and organizational learning during the identify needs stage of the LDC.

Summary

- DNA should be approached from the perspective of the organization being a system, where the different parts of the organization are interdependent upon each other.
- The learning practitioner is responsible for developing knowledge and understanding about how the organizational system operates.
- The model of organizational balance provides a map to navigate specific elements of organizational performance from the perspective of a people-centered ecosystem.

- If development interventions work against the organization's human ecosystem, then resistance, drag, and natural barriers will affect performance.
- There are a myriad of data types available, and for the analysis to demonstrate areas where usefulness or advantage can be achieved.
- Dialogic data collection methods provide soft, vitality, proficiency, and power data, which can be analyzed using qualitative data analysis techniques.
- Diagnostic data collection methods provide hard, stakeholder, proficiency, and market data, which can be analyzed using quantitative data analysis techniques.
- The DNA process can result in positive improvements in organizational performance and organizational learning during the identify needs stage of the LDC.

CHAPTER 6

Delivering the Business Case for Learning and Development

Depending on the organization in which the learning practitioner works, it may be necessary to provide leaders with a business case for learning interventions. If a strategic management approach to learning and development is going to be adopted, then building a business case for learning and development interventions is a necessary component. However, regardless of whether a business case is required or not, it is recommended that learning practitioners become comfortable with examining learning and development from a commercial perspective. Furthermore, if the learning practitioner wants to change the conversation about budgets from being allocated a budget to one where programs are fully funded because business leaders believe they will deliver a return on investment (ROI), then being able to write a robust business case is fundamental to learning and development practice.

A business case forces the learning practitioner to think beyond the operational requirements of the learning and development function and consider the reasons why the proposed intervention adds value to the organization and supports the organization's goals. Furthermore, it changes the focus to a client-facing consideration of the reasons why business leaders will resist or support the proposal. A business case provides the opportunity for the learning practitioner to establish credibility among business leaders, demonstrate their expertise in the field of learning and development, develop their knowledge and experience of evaluating the external and internal environment, and cultivate a capability to establish learning and development strategies in response to diagnostic data.

A robust business case contains a number of facets; it provides a rationale for why a learning and development intervention or program is needed within the context of supporting the organization in achieving its organizational strategic goal. A second component involves explaining what business problem or opportunity exists which can be resolved by a learning and development intervention, with a review of the benefits and costs of different options available. The final element is to provide a recommendation for action.

The first consideration in writing a business case is to determine what it is that business leaders require for a positive decision to be made regarding the allocation of financial resources. This will include considerations regarding the financial impact of the proposed intervention including the following:

- Cost outlay versus cash flow
- ROI
- Payback period
- Performance outcomes
- Impact on operation improvement
- Potential revenue impact
- The risk of failure

The task of the learning practitioner is to convince business leaders to allocate resources to learning and development by demonstrating that their proposed solution has a high likelihood of success. This means that the business case must include key pieces of information, which demonstrate that the learning practitioner has considered all the success factors pertinent to the circumstances including the following:

- Evidence that the solution has been employed successfully before
- An analysis of critical success and failure factors
- The impact of environmental factors that are pertinent to the proposed intervention
- Learning and development resource availability including talent, capability, technology, and capacity

- The financial impacts including revenue, payback, and cost
- Measure of success
- Calculation of anticipated ROI
- How the intervention or program contributes to the achievement of the organization's strategy
- Possible additional funding, for example, government schemes

Sections in a Business Case

There are plenty of resources regarding formats for the development of a business cases and some organizations have standard templates that are used which should be adopted if available. Below is an outline of sections, which make up a comprehensive business case.

Section 1—Executive Summary

Although this is the first section of the business case, it will be the final section that is written. The executive summary summarizes the other sections of the document and briefly outlines the problem or opportunity, which the learning and development intervention will resolve, a recommended solution, with a concise overview of alternatives and the reasons they have been discarded, and finally a plan for implementation. A detailed implementation plan can be included as an appendix to the business case to explain major program phases, resource deployment, and program management.

Section 2—Business Problem or Opportunity

This section sets the scene for business leaders by describing what the business need is for a learning and development intervention. This can be defined in terms of a problem or opportunity that needs to be resolved. The use of hard statistical data gathered during the development needs analysis (DNA) provides evidence of the current situation and provides the basis for developing the ROI in regards to identifying the areas that performance outcomes, operation improvement, or impact on business results can be delivered.

Section 3—Environmental Analysis

This section contains pertinent data collected during the DNA phase, which provide evidence to support the conclusions drawn and establish the need for a learning and development intervention. The data analysis provided needs to be focused on the areas, which relate specifically to the identified business problem or opportunity. For example:

- Cultural change needed to deliver the organization strategy
- Issues in specific areas of the business operations
- Turnover or absence data indicating managerial development needs
- Areas of the organization where a skills shortage is having an impact on operations
- Opportunities created by the introduction of new technology
- Competitor activity that requires a shift in service delivery
- Training requirements driven by regulatory or legal changes

Section 4—Problem Analysis

This section involves clarifying the underlying problem or opportunity, which will be addressed through the implementation of the learning and development intervention and the organizational impact of the problem or opportunity. This may include a clear deadline for when the problem needs to be resolved especially with the introduction of a new regulatory framework or where a specific opportunity is only available during a set time frame. The analysis will also include what has caused the problem to exist, or evidence that the opportunity is real in order to contextualize the problem for the business leaders. Finally, evidence will be provided outlining the impact that addressing the problem or opportunity will have on the organization.

Section 5—Options

This section explores the alternate options that could be utilized to resolve the identified problem or opportunity. Each solution option will be described alongside a benefit analysis, estimated costs and possible funding sources, feasibility study, risk analysis, and assumptions. It is worth noting that doing nothing is an option that needs to be included. At this stage, it may be difficult to ascertain what benefit may be derived from doing something in regards to a learning and development intervention. A good rule of thumb is to propose a 1 percent improvement either in terms of increased profitability or cost efficiency. High priority issues should also be identified in regards to factors, which might prevent the proposed solution from delivering the identified benefits.

Section 6—Recommended Option

This section is a simple tabulation of the various options presented and ranking all the options against the benefits, costs, feasibility, risks, and impact identified in Section 5. This section also includes a brief summary explaining the main reasons why the option is being recommended ahead of the other options.

Summary

- If a strategic management approach to learning and development is going to be adopted, then building a business case for learning and development interventions is a necessary component.
- A business case changes the conversation from budget allocation to one where programs are fully funded because business leaders believe they will deliver a ROI.
- The first consideration in writing a business case is to determine what it is that business leaders require for a positive decision to be made regarding the allocation of financial resources.
- The task of the learning practitioner is to convince business leaders to allocate resources to learning and development by demonstrating that their proposed solution has a high likelihood of success.
- A comprehensive business case includes executive summary, business problem or opportunity, environmental analysis, problem analysis, options, and recommended option.

CHAPTER 7

Design Elements for Sustainable Organizational Effectiveness

If the learning and development function is to contribute the performance gap between current state and future state, then a fundamental element is that of change, whether changing behavior or capability. The learning practitioner will need to incorporate design elements that support change, and help to ensure that developed capabilities are embedded and sustained over the long term.

Very often when organizations approach strategic challenges relating to organizational effectiveness, their focus is on how things can be improved from a process perspective. This focus is quite rightly exploring how things can be done more efficiently within the business and eliminating waste. The development of total quality management (TQM), business process re-engineering (BPR), and lean six sigma methodologies has dominated change management programs. However, what many change management programs miss are the human processes that sit alongside the operational (product and service) processes that exist within the business. What a systems theory approach reminds us is that the organizational effectiveness is the result of a healthy interaction and functioning interdependencies between both the human processes and the operational processes. It is possible for an organization to have an inefficient operational process, which people will work around and deliver organizational performance or have an efficient operational process that is ineffective because of poor employee engagement. Human processes in organizations matter because it is people who operate the operational processes.

Improving Organizational Health through Human Processes

Social Construction Theory highlights that the organization as an entity is a product of dialogue about the organization by organizational players. Therefore; if an organization needs to change its operational processes, it is also obliged to change the way those processes are discussed and understood within the organization by the people who use them. This may, at first glance, appear fanciful and time consuming, but since there is a general consensus that 70 percent of change programs fail to deliver their stated financial outcomes, the investment is worthwhile.

How individuals and teams communicate is an ongoing battle for many organizational leaders. However, for many organizations the focus is on channels of communication and messaging content rather than on enriching dialogue between individuals and groups. A key design element that needs to be included in development interventions is the creation of a space where focused and positive dialogue within and between individuals, teams, and groups can take place.

Following World War II, Kurt Lewin contributed seminal research to the field of Group Dynamics, which is concerned with determining the laws underlying group behavior. Group Dynamics provides the theoretical foundation for the learning practitioner to understand how groups form and structured. It explains the interaction and behavioral processes that occur and impact upon the effectiveness of the group functioning. Lewin (1947) introduced two key ideas that are fundamental to being able to impact group processes through an intervention: interdependence of fate and task interdependence.

Interdependence of fate refers to the realization by people that their fate depends upon whole group success. This realization results in:

- Group cohesion,
- Individuals being proactive in their responsibility in delivering group goals, and
- Group members acting to support overall group welfare.

However, Lewin suggested that Interdependence of fate was a weak form of interdependence in many groups. Instead, from Lewin's perspective, task interdependence was a more significant factor in driving collaboration toward successful outcomes and the achievement of group goals. However, task Interdependence can be negative or positive. Negative interdependence, or competition can lead to win:lose outcomes, however, positive task interdependence can result in positive win:win outcomes as a result of the group operating as a dynamic whole.

In designing interventions, learning practitioners should:

- Pay attention to group dynamics and the powerful forces within the groups,
- Identify existing rules that create the current organizational reality and change them to create movement,
- Plan the mix of people involved in diagnostic and intervention events in order to shift forces and facilitate change,
- Provide a desirable direction or "best way" for group members to change toward,
- Facilitate and guide change and periods of transition,
- Generate motivation for change before attempting change,
- Help participants to re-examine many cherished assumptions about self, relationships, and the group as part of the process, and
- Use a process of voluntary and responsible participation to help people learn about democracy within group functioning.

Individual Self-renewal

Gardner (1964) argues that excellence and high standards are not enough to drive forward toward success. For an organization to achieve renewal, then individuals within the organization must renew themselves, continuing to develop their capacity to learn and grow. The learning and development cycle must include regular opportunities for individuals to self-renew. Opportunities are myriad and although strategic talent may benefit from greater levels of investment and resource in self-renewal opportunities, individuals seeking self-renewal should, where possible, have the freedom to pursue their own growth and learning. In this respect, the learning and development function should focus on promoting the benefits of a culture of learning within the organizational setting and provide easy access, cheap, or free self-renewal opportunities such as online learning portals, learning zones, or simply support in guiding people toward learning opportunities. Too often employees are denied time off to attend workshops or participate in learning opportunities that their own manager has highlighted as part of the annual review or in a personal development plan (PDP). Learning is seen as noncore activity or a nice to have, instead of an added value pursuit. Evaluating the ROI from self-renewal activities is very often too difficult or time consuming to capture centrally but a simple calculation of output (what's been delivered) versus input (cost of delivery) can help the learning practitioner demonstrate the extent of learning investment, whether formally or informally, happening within the organization.

Action Learning

Revans (1972) introduced the concept of Action Learning as a structured approach where participants working in small group can learn from experience and take action in order to foster learning in the workplace. The benefit of Action Learning is that it creates a discipline of reflection in action, enabling participants to learn from what they do in order to improve the way they work. In addition, Action Learning delivers workplace solutions to real time work issues. Voluntary sets of groups of small groups of six members or less commit to meeting regularly to reflect on workplace issues. Set members take turns to be the presenter offering a workplace challenge for discussion. Set members help the presenter to work through the problem by employing encouraging, but probing, questioning. As the presenter develops an answer to the workplace issue, an action plan is created, again supported by the set members. The primary focus of the Action Learning Set is for individual to learn from experience and then applying their learning immediately when they return to the workplace. The action learning set becomes a group of people who will hold the presenter to account for implementing the action plan at their next meeting.

Knowledge Management

Knowledge management (KM) refers to the organization's ability to manage crucial knowledge required for the achievement of an organization's strategic goal, and necessary to ensure the smooth execution of the organization's operations. Nonaka and Takeuchi (1995) introduced the concept of KM to describe how knowledge can be transferred within the organization and to develop the ability to use the knowledge, which exists within the organization to add value to the organization.

Nonaka introduced two types of knowledge which can be converted and be developed as part of a continuous learning process:

- **Tacit Knowledge:** Subjective knowledge developed through experience, best described as know-how.
- **Explicit Knowledge:** Objective knowledge that can be codified, passed on, or taught to others.

Tacit knowledge can be transferred through social learning processes, specifically through experiential learning and dialogic interventions, which enable individuals to share experience between individuals, whereas exchanging relevant material can convey explicit knowledge. Learning and development interventions can provide processes to transfer tacit knowledge and enable individuals to internalize ideas through action or reflection.

Creativity and Innovation

Gurteen (1998) argues that KM is an important discipline within organizations since applying new knowledge results in creativity and innovation, which can have a significant impact on the way and organization conducts business. In addition to the know-how highlighted by Nonaka and Takeuchi (1995), Gurteen (1998) suggests that know-why is essential for knowledge to become productive and for creativity to be developed in regards to reinventing know-how.

For KM to have any impact on creativity and innovation, individual competence must be developed in order that knowledge can be disseminated across the organization and leveraged to deliver organizational strategic goals. Therefore, the learning practitioner must consider not just how to manage knowledge within the business to ensure that knowledge is not lost but also how knowledge, and therefore creativity and innovation, can be nurtured. The development of forums for collaboration and the creation of space in which individuals, teams, and functions have the opportunity to learn, influence, and activate their knowledge is a significant element of learning and development design, which can contribute to sustainable organizational effectiveness.

Summary

- A fundamental element of closing the performance gap is that of change, whether changing behavior or capability.
- Organizational effectiveness is the result of a healthy interaction and functioning interdependencies between both the human processes and the operational processes.
- A key design element is the creation of a space where focused and positive dialogue within and between individuals, teams, and groups can take place.
- Group Dynamics explains the interaction and behavioral processes that occur and impact upon the effectiveness of the group functioning.
- Positive task interdependence can result in positive win: Win outcomes as a result of the group operating as a dynamic whole.
- Individuals seeking self-renewal should, where possible, have the freedom to pursue their own growth and learning.
- KM refers to the organization's ability to manage crucial knowledge required for the achievement of an organization's strategic goal, and necessary to ensure the smooth execution of the organization's operations.
- For KM to have any impact on creativity and innovation, individual competence must be developed.

CHAPTER 8

Learning and Development Audit

The word audit very often conjures up images of the Gestapo arriving to torture individuals of a team until they have made a confession regarding all of the mistakes the department has made. However, it is imperative that the learning and development function is a department that leads by example. As learning practitioners we must be willing to proactively learn from what has happened, both good and bad, and respond to that learning by developing, changing, and renewing to become more effective and more efficient.

Given the speed of change in the organizational environment, regular evaluation of what, how, and why are essential to managing expectations of the business leaders and demonstrating the value that the learning and development function is delivering. Too often, learning practitioners expect business leaders to know the value they are delivering without disclosing what it is, exactly, that the learning and development function actually does. For most employees their only knowledge of what the learning and development function is doing is the few workshops they are invited to attend. For many others the workings and machinations of learning and development are little more than voodoo magic and result in business leaders wondering why the learning and development budget and team are as big as they are or why the function has a budget at all. What exactly is it that learning and development do? This can lead to false assumptions and an inaccurate belief that learning and development is pink and fluffy and somewhat detached from the realities of the day-to-day business of running the organization.

Therefore; a learning and development audit goes beyond simply evaluating the efficiency of the learning and development function, and assures senior leaders they are getting value for money. An audit promotes the professional management of the learning and development function and the professionalism of the learning practitioner. It provides a benchmark against which improvements can be made, both in systems and practices, and aids growth and expansion into different areas, going beyond transactional learning and development practices into the realms of learning and development acting as a trusted adviser on the development of the organization's most valued resource, its people.

In Chapter 1, typologies of evaluation were explored. A comprehensive evaluation of the learning and development function is required to conduct a learning and development audit. This will examine the following:

- **Strategy:** In what ways are the long-term and short-term plan vertically aligned with the organizational strategy and horizontally aligned to the human resource (HR) strategy? What evidence is there that the learning and development strategy is fit for purpose? Where and how can the strategy be improved?
- **Strategic Planning:** What value does the learning and development strategic planning bring? How efficient is the strategic planning process? Who is involved in strategic planning? Who should be involved in strategic planning in the future? What improvements can be made to the strategic planning process? How can these improvements be implemented?
- **Structure:** What evidence is there that the functional design of learning and development ensures that interventions are delivered by the right person, with the right skills at the right time? In what ways does the structure of the learning and development function support business needs and ensure that learning practitioners are close to the business? How is collaboration and cooperation encouraged and enabled? What evidence is there that the structure flexible enough to react to business changes? How does the structure impact the attitudes

of internal customers toward learning and the learning and development function? Where and how can the structure be improved?

- **Systems:** What evidence is there that the learning and development systems support the learning and development cycle (LDC)? In what ways can processes be described as efficient? How do systems enable the internal clients to interact with the learning and development team effectively? Where and how can systems and processes be improved?

- **Practices:** What evidence is there that the learning and development practices are fit for purpose? How does learning practitioner continuously improve their practices? What methods are used to keep up to date with the latest development in learning and development? How are new developments shared and where appropriately incorporated? What pockets of excellence exist and how can these be shared among the wider team? Where and how can learning and development practices be improved?

Intervention Value Evaluation

The format for a learning and development audit requires the learning practitioner to look inward to the workings of their own function and focus on what has been delivered in terms of work and the processes of work that are taking place. It includes an examination of the working relationship between team members as well as the outcomes of the work the team has delivered. The focus is on value of task outcomes as well as the efficiency of the processes that produce those outcomes. It is possible to calculate the value of outcomes produced by the learning and development function by using the value equation.

$$\frac{\text{Quality}}{\text{Cost} \times \text{Time}} = \text{Value}$$

Quality in the value equation is an assessment of the value added by an enhancement that participants achieve either in skills, knowledge, or ability as a result of their higher education. Quality is organization specific, but can be captured and monetized by the learning and development function.

Energy Transformation Value Evaluation Case Study

- **Situation:** Through discussions with managers about "what will make the biggest difference," the focus was on improving customer satisfaction, which was below industry average.
- **Task:** Following an investigation into the existing customer satisfaction, development areas identified included empowerment to solve problem, breaking siloes to have one company working and developing commercial thinking in the service engineers.
- **Action:** Delivered a diagnostic theater of inquiry for managers. Observed and interviewed engineers. Ran Design group included members of the target participants and piloted program. Showcased workshop to Board of Directors to gain buy in and support required for organizationwide intervention, especially realizing staff to attend workshops. Delivered coaching customer service for managers prior to workshop roll out.
- **Result:** Delivered 32 days of facilitated workshops with over 204 participants, 2-day workshop each.
  - Customer satisfaction improved by 47 percent, above industry standard, and was maintained for over 12 months, £200,100 additional revenue was attributed to this increase.
  - Breakdowns reduced by 13 percent, saving £205,000.
  - Self-reporting of applying learning in practice resulted in an identified benefit of £804,000 in 12 months.
  - Materials and external facilitator costs were £90,000 for the program.
  - *Cost based on an average salary of four × learning practitioners of £30,000 per annum, 290 working days per annum.
  - Time is based on a six-month LDC.

$$\frac{£200,100 + £205,000 + £804,000}{(£621 + £414^{*}) \times 145} = \frac{£1,209,100}{£150,075} = 8.06$$

Value of Learning Experience Delivery

Alignment to strategic priorities can be generated around the principle that the quality of learning and development interventions must take into account not only learning outcomes, but also the delivery of learning experience.

It is possible to calculate the contribution that learning opportunities make to employee commitment, engagement, and productivity. Although not an exact science, rough estimates can be provided which can contribute to decision making both within the business in terms of understanding the value that the learning and development function delivers, and also within the function itself to decide which intervention activity is creating the most value.

The value that learning experience delivery can contribute to the organization can be measured using Reichheld (2003) Net Promoter Score (Figure 8.1) by asking participants in learning interventions one question: How likely is it that you would recommend this learning experience to a friend or colleague?

Although passive scores do not affect the overall net promoter score, they are counted as part of the total number of respondents.

On a monthly or quarterly basis, the accumulated net promoter response results, over a variety of learning interventions, can then be plotted against the organization's revenue growth rate and other identified key people performance metrics identified in Chapter 3. This will provide

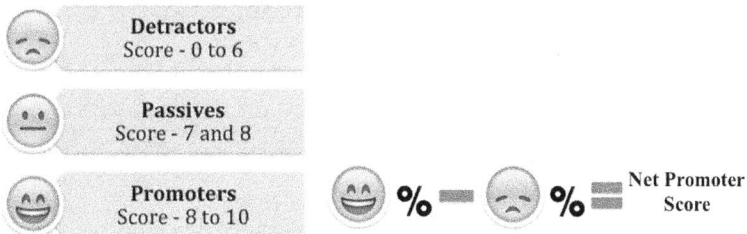

Figure 8.1 Net promoter score

the learning and development function with the data for a longitudinal correlation analysis between participant satisfaction and organizational performance. It is also possible for the learning and development function to examine the relationship between participant responses and actual career development, turnover or absence data.

Outcome Evaluation of the Learning and Development Function

In addition to a comprehensive evaluation of the value that the learning and development function is delivering via their operational effectiveness, it is also possible to develop an outcome evaluation of the way short- and long-term changes in group behavior of the learning and development team work outcomes are delivered. This provides an evaluation of the group dynamics in regards to interdependence of task. Metrics that can be utilized as a value outcome include the following;

- Line manager time spent resolving conflict within the function
- Line manager time spent resolving conflict between function and other functions
- Line manager time spent resolving conflict between function and external suppliers
- Frequency of workgroup conflict and the time to resolve issues
- Process improvements as a result of workgroup collaboration
- Longitudinal mapping of team performance improvement

Harmonious Community Outcomes Case Study

- **Situation/Task:** Learning and development teams in a global organization were siloed. Communication and sharing best practice was limited, resulting in duplication of effort, blame, and misunderstanding.
- **Action:** Introduced communities of practice, learning buddy, and job shadowing program as part of team building

intervention. Established learning zone on the intranet and introduced a learning and development chat forum. Introduced certified practitioner standard.

- **Result:** Increased networking and one organization thinking in the learning and development team. Recorded £146,000 of improvements in productivity in six months. Some communities of practice important to future innovation generation in key strategic areas.

Summary

- Regular evaluation of what, how, and why are essential to managing expectations of the business leaders and demonstrating the value that the learning and development function is delivering.
- An audit promotes the professional management of the learning and development function and the professionalism of the learning practitioner.
- A comprehensive evaluation of the learning and development function is required to conduct a learning and development audit.
- It is possible to calculate the value of outcomes produced by the learning and development function by using the value equation Quality/Cost × Time = Value.
- An outcome evaluation measures the short- and long-term changes within group behavior of the learning and development team to provide an evaluation of the group dynamics in regards to interdependence of task.

CHAPTER 9

Calculating Return on Investment

The primary purpose of calculating return on investment (ROI) is to demonstrate the value of learning and development to the organization, and provide a financial summation of the contribution that learning and development has made toward the achievement of the organization's strategic priorities. For this reason, what financial outcome and advantage variables are chosen to calculate ROI are specific to the organization in which the learning practitioner operates. The formula for ROI, however, is the same regardless of the organization.

$$\frac{\text{Net Benefits}}{\text{Costs}} \times 100 = \text{ROI}(\%)$$

Therefore; in order to evaluate the ROI for any intervention, the learning practitioner needs to know how much the intervention cost and what the intervention delivered in terms of net benefits to the organization.

Organizational Husbandry ROI Case Study

- **Situation:** Request to retrain 400 strong commercial teams on the use of a customer relationship management system because there were costly adjustments every month as the result of incorrect data input.
- **Task:** To enhance user adoption of the new system and drive positive behavior change to ensure right first time data entry. Stakeholder analysis revealed that the functional heads were not using the systems and duplicating work by asking

employees to deliver the information outside of the system. Diagnostic demonstrated that the users knew the processes they should be following but found short cuts to save time.

- **Action:** Worked alongside various departments in the business to understand where the issues were impacting the business, plus the IT department on system updates. Delivered one to one coaching and training for functional head and 18 × 2 day business workshops delivered by the functional heads supported by facilitators.
- **Result:** Reinforced culture of good data input.
  - Data variance dropped by 62 percent, leading to a £9 million improvement in profit contribution in the six weeks following the workshop.
  - Forecast accuracy improved by 92 percent reducing costs from £2.7 million to £404,000 and resulting in fewer invoice queries.
  - Materials, room, technology, and facilitator costs were £2.5 million for the program.
  - Cost based on an average salary over 290 working days per annum for:
    - Nine months' time for two × learning practitioners at £45,000 average salary per annum
    - Two days' time for 400 × Commercial Team at £50,000 average salary per annum
    - Ten days' time for six × Functional Heads at £100,000 average salary per annum

$$\frac{£9,000,000 + £2,296,000}{£2,500,000 + £67,500 + £137,931 + £20,689}$$

$$= \frac{£11,296,000}{£2,726,120} \times 100 = 414.36\%$$

Financial Outcome and Advantage Variables

In regards to calculating the benefits delivered by an intervention, there are myriad of variables, which the learning practitioner can identify and use to measure financial outcomes and advantages, which contribute to organizational performance. The finance department is a good source of financial outcome and advantage variables and support in terms of how to calculate the variable. The metrics used to measure outcomes will be dependent on the organization's strategic priorities and performance metrics. Table 9.1 shows a small sample of financial outcome and advantage

Table 9.1 *Financial outcome and advantage variables*

Variable	Outcome or Advantage	Calculation
Sales performance	Improved organizational performance, revenue, and profit	Calculate the benefit of improved sales performance by measuring the profit contribution of additional sales in a given time period.
Process improvement	Improved cost efficiency	Calculate the benefit of trimming process times by measuring the time saved in employee salary multiplied by the number of employees doing this job.
Productivity	Measure the change in productivity	Select a measure of productivity, e.g., units produced, customers served, projects completed, and so on. Subtract the starting productivity figure from the end productivity figure in a given time period. Divide the value of change by the starting value and multiply by 100 to calculate a percentage change in productivity.
Cost to acquire a customer	Focuses on the effectiveness of efforts to expand the customer base	Divide all the costs spent on marketing and sales promotion by the number of new customers acquired in the same period.
Customer retention rate	Provides an indication of customer loyalty and quality of customer service delivered by your employees	Calculate the number of remaining customers by subtracting the number of new customers acquired during a time period by the number of the customers at the end of that period. Divide by the number of customers at the start of that period and multiply by 100 to get a customer retention rate percentage.
Revenue Renewal rates	Focuses on the revenue retained rather than customers. Provides an indication of increases in share of wallet, upsell or cross sell, or revenue growth.	Base the calculation on a customer cohort basis with each time period representing a new customer cohort. Measure the percentage of revenue retained over the prior time period.

variables that may be used, but this is in no way a complete or comprehensive list.

Return on Expectation

In addition to ROI calculations, return on expectation (ROE) is a meaningful way to measure learning and development outcomes and advantages within the business. Expectations are success measures, which have been expressed in terms of what the future state organization will look and feel like by the people in the business. It is a less tangible elucidation of how things will be different when we get to the strategic destination, and therefore is based on a long-term evaluation of what success will look like. Examples include the following:

- We get more done in business meetings
- People come up with more ideas and share those ideas
- There's less conflict
- People complete their actions from a meeting
- There's a respect for other people in time keeping or attending meetings
- There is an increase in face-to-face conversation
- There is a reduction in copying everyone into every e-mail conversation
- People collaborate more, we're working as one organization instead of separate fiefdoms

Although ROE measures don't provide an evaluation measure in the sense of having a financial outcome or advantage, they do express a cultural shift or change which is seen as an advantage or outcome that makes the organization a better place to work, and therefore has a value to the key stakeholders who are seeking a change in the way in which employees interact and work within the organization. Capturing expectations at the start of the learning and development cycle (LDC) enables the learning practitioner to communicate an evaluation of additional value factors, which although are not financial, are valued by the organization's stakeholders.

Reporting Results

Calculating ROI and ROE is only an input to a process of demonstrating the value of learning and development to the organization. Reporting the results of learning and development training audit, ROI, and ROE completes the LDC. Even if added value results are produced, they aren't always shared with key decision makers or stakeholders within the business. Having relationships with organizational leaders and key stakeholders is important. Communicating results helps build those relationships and supports the development of an organizationwide understanding of what exactly it is that the learning and development function does, and, of course, what value it delivers.

Depending on the size of the organization and function, monthly, quarterly, and annual reporting of ROI, ROE, and activity are an essential output and input of the LDC. Not only does reporting results build momentum for programs and projects being designed and implemented, but it opens a communication channel which increases the richness of diagnostic and dialogic data collection for identifying needs, making the process iterative.

Summary

- The primary purpose of calculating ROI is to demonstrate the value of learning and development to the organization.
- ROI provides a financial summation of the contribution that learning and development has made toward the achievement of the organization's strategic priorities.
- In order to evaluate the ROI, the learning practitioner needs to know the costs and the net benefits of the intervention.
- Expectations are an expression of success measures as to what the future state organization will look and feel like.
- Communicating results helps build stakeholder relationships and develops an organizationwide understanding of what value the learning and development function delivers.
- Reporting results is an iterative process, which increases the richness of diagnostic and dialogic data collection for identifying needs.

CHAPTER 10

Challenging Attitudes to Learning and Development

The driving force behind designing learning and development for return on investment is that too often learning and development is a function that is relegated to a cost on the organization's balance sheet. This placement of investment in the development of employees as cost burden is curious when considered in the context of other forms of capital investment, which is measured in terms of value being created.

However, business leaders are beginning to change their attitude as to the competitive advantage provided by their human resource, specifically in regards to the increasing requirement for organizations to deliver new knowledge, creativity, and innovation to survive the fast moving, complex, and globalized marketplace.

The organizational environment of the 21st century provides an opportunity for the learning and development function to evolve the field and utilize the wide range of theory, practitioner knowledge, and skills to support organizations and their employees to adapt and respond to the environmental forces effectively. In addition to developing professional knowledge and skills, learning practitioners must also develop a clear understanding of the commercial aspects of their organization in order to integrate and systematically align learning and development with organizational strategic goals. Importantly, learning practitioners can impact organizational performance, growth, and innovation by maturing the learning and development cycle (LDC) to apply a proactive strategic approach and reducing reactive activity, which focuses on symptoms and reactive approaches.

For many learning and development functions, the transactional training delivery, in regards to statutory or compliance-driven training, is being outsourced or converted into e-learning platforms that can be managed by learning management systems. This frees up the learning practitioner to focus upon partnering with the organization to deliver learning, which is contextually relevant and activity which develops the people resource in key strategic areas. To stay relevant, learning practitioners must increase their awareness of the business environment and develop business acumen, negotiation skills, and communication skills in addition to expanding their professional specialism and learning and development toolkit. Innovations in learning techniques and methodology must be delivered alongside a learning and development agenda, which contributes positively to improvements in business change management, employee agility, and long-term organizational growth. The development of a robust learning and development strategy focused on supporting the organization to deliver today's strategic plans while preparing for the organization's future means that the learning practitioner must be able to demonstrate strategic and creative capability, while being agile and accountable in responding to the complex and changing needs of the organization.

The shift from training as a business cost to learning and development delivering a return on investment is provided by learning practitioners who understand the role of learning and development in the wider organizational context and the delivery of a range of value-added initiatives.

The Value Can Learning and Development Add

In Chapter 4, a range of metrics were offered as possible measures of success to evaluate learning and development. Before designing and delivering learning and development, it is essential that the learning practitioner and the business leaders are clear as to what benefit the intervention will deliver to the organization. This means quite simply that either the learning and development intervention fixes a problem or equips the organization to take advantage of presenting opportunities. The value this can add to the organization is twofold. Either the value added results in additional growth and/or profit or it drives cost efficiencies. In this respect, learning and development enhances the organization, improves organizational effectiveness, and develops employee capability supporting sustainable performance. This is the story that reporting ROI delivers to business leaders about learning and development. This is how choosing metrics, which matter to the organization, enables the learning practitioner to challenge attitudes to learning and development.

Stakeholder Management

The learning practitioner must become competent at managing key stakeholders who have an influence on prevailing attitudes toward learning and development within the organization. The identification of key stakeholders is the beginning of the stakeholder management process. To commence the process, the learning practitioner is required to examine the priorities of each stakeholder and understand what they want from learning and development. This process could be formal, but simply establishing contact, and regular review meetings sharing progress reports and discussing what next over a cup of coffee is often more powerful in managing stakeholders. The focus is on understanding their needs and being responsive in meeting them, while at the same time managing expectations. It is not possible to please everyone all the time, being clear on what can't be done is as important as explaining what will be done.

Stakeholder management is a two-way procedure because the learning practitioner will need to also be explicit about what is needed from each stakeholder. This may be, for example, garnering commitment regarding sponsorship of programs, which directly address their needs, allocation of financial resource, support in ensuring participants are released to attend interventions, or the provision of information.

Creating Proactive Advocacy

To truly challenge attitudes toward learning and development within the organization, the aim must be for the learning and development to progress stakeholders, and especially senior leaders, from passive acceptance of the existence of learning and development within the organization to the development of a core group of advocates who are passionate about the role that learning and development has to play within the organization. This is the ultimate goal of stakeholder management.

Providing a substantive business case for learning and development to demonstrate how organizational problems or opportunities can be resolved by a learning and development intervention builds credibility and a connection between the learning and development function and the rest of the business. Delivering a tangible return on investment, which demonstrates a business result and real benefit to the business, squares the circle.

However, creating proactive advocacy goes beyond financial calculations, it requires the learning practitioner to convince stakeholders to buy in to the narrative regarding the purpose that learning and development plays within the organization. The following recommendations are made to nurture advocacy:

- **Heart Felt Communication:** Avoid communication that lacks feeling, instead the learning practitioner should share their passion, and deliver communication which is thoughtful, clear, and authentic.
- **Personal Interaction:** Abandon e-mail in favor of engaging in conversation in person. It is easy to ignore an e-mail, but it is hard to ignore someone when they are in person.
- **Get People Talking:** Do not be afraid to create a scene or disturb the environment by creating a buzz about what is happening in learning and development. Learn about marketing and employ some of the tools and techniques to create a brand message internally.
- **Be Thankful:** Whether it is to the receptionist who takes deliveries of workshop materials in the office building, a caretaker who moves tables and chairs for a facilitator, a program sponsor who shows their support, or a participant who provides valuable feedback. Saying thank you, in person, in writing, or even occupied by a small gift of appreciation will encourage continued advocacy.
- **Be Transparent:** Sometimes, mistakes will be made and interventions will fail to deliver the anticipated ROI. It is

not the failure that will be remembered but the response to it. Practice continuous professional development, learn from feedback, respond to criticism with a learning mindset, and develop a response that will fix the situation.

Designing learning and development for ROI creates a cultural shift within the learning and development function, toward a coherent value-added approach which in turn will deliver changing attitudes to learning and development. The final piece of the puzzle to creating a new perception of learning and development is to manage the communication of the added value delivered and increasing the visibility of the contribution that learning and development is making to the organization and the achievement of its strategic goals.

Summary

- Business leaders are beginning to change their attitude as to the competitive advantage provided by their human resource.
- Learning practitioners must increase their awareness of the business environment and develop business acumen, negotiation, and communication skills.
- The learning practitioner must be able to demonstrate strategic and creative capability, while being agile and accountable in responding to the complex and changing needs of the organization.
- Value-added learning and development either results in additional growth and/or profit or it drives cost efficiencies.
- Being clear on what can't be done is as important as explaining what will be done.
- Creating proactive advocacy requires the learning practitioner to convince stakeholders to buy in to the narrative regarding the purpose that learning and development plays within the organization.

Conclusion

The purpose of this book is to demystify the process of calculating return on investment (ROI), explain how to use the formula and enable learning practitioners to understand that it is possible to use existing mechanisms to deliver a ROI analysis and develop a commercial mindset by designing learning and development *for* ROI. In today's organizational environment, where a strong economic agenda and focus on shareholder value is the order of the day, ROI is ignored only by those who do not care for a secure future of learning and development within the organization.

This book offers a brief overview of both theory and practical framework. The theoretical underpinning provides a signpost for further exploration but is not fully comprehensive, and the encouragement in this conclusion is to investigate further as to how the theories and research about human and group dynamic processes and self-renewal can be utilized in intervention design. As with all frameworks, their practicality is delivered through their use. If the learning and development function develops its practices and employs some of the tools presented in these pages, then there will be a shift in perception of learning and development being a function that is a cost to the organization, to it being a function which is central to delivering value-added activities for the organization.

Owning the Numbers

For numerous human resource (HR) and learning practitioners, numbers are a beastly nemesis, sent to disturb their sensibilities. The central proposition of this book is that it is essential that learning practitioners get used to numbers and use numbers to demonstrate the value that is being added. Why? Instinct frames investment in HR development as an obvious contributor to the achievement of the organization's strategy and improvements to organizational health. However, avoiding a fully costed business case, or proof that the investment in interventions is delivering business results, leaves the learning practitioner relying on an enlightened business leader to make an investment of scarce organizational resources on faith. In general, the world rarely works on faith and resources have to be allocated according to those activities that deliver the best ROI. It is imperative that the learning practitioner owns the numbers to enable them to bid for adequate resources to support the organization's strategic ambitions.

Summary

- ROI is ignored only by those who do not care for a secure future of learning and development within the organization.
- Avoiding proof that interventions are delivering business results relies on an enlightened business leader making investment decisions on faith.
- The learning and development function can be perceived as being central to delivering value-added activities for the organization.
- It is imperative that the learning practitioner owns the numbers to enable them to bid for adequate resources.

References

Arnold, J. and Silvester, J. 2005. *Work Psychology: Understanding Human Behaviour in the Workplace*. Upper Saddle River, NJ: Pearson Education.

Berger, P. L. and Luckmann, T. 1966. *The Social Construction of Reality*. New York, NY: Random House.

Bertalanffy, L. 1950. *An Outline of General System Theory*. British Journal of the Philosophy of Science, 1, pp. 134–165.

Cairns, T. D. 2012. *Overcoming the Challenges to Developing an ROI for Training and Development*. Employment Relations Today, 39, no. 3, pp. 23–27.

Cheung-Judge, M. and Holbeche, L. 2015. *Organization Development: A Practitioner's Guide for OD and HR*. London: Kogan Page.

Collins, J. 2001. *Good to Great*. New York, NY: Random House Business.

Covey, S. 2004. *Seven Habits of High Effective People*. New York, NY: Simon & Schuster.

Covey, S. 2015. *The 4 Disciplines of Execution: Achieving Your Wildly Important Goals*. New York, NY: Simon & Schuster.

Garavan, T. N. 2007. *A Strategic Perspective on Human Resource Development*. Advances in Developing Human Resources, 9, no. 1, p. 11.

Gardner, J. 1964. *Self-Renewal: The Individual and the Innovative Society*. New York, NY: Joanna Cotler Books.

Guest, D. E. 1997. *Human Resource Management and Performance: A review and Research Agenda*. International Journal of Human Resource Management, 8, no. 3, pp. 263–276.

Gurteen, D. 1998. *Knowledge Management and Creativity*. Journal of Knowledge Management, 2, no. 1, pp. 25–37.

Ho, M. 2016. *Conduct Learning Evaluation that Make a Difference*. TD: Talent Development Magazine, ATD, 70, no. 7, pp. 20–20.

Lewin, K. 1947. *Frontiers in Group Dynamics: Concept, Method and Reality in Social Science; Social Equilibria and Social Change*. Human Relations, 1, no. 5, pp. 5–41.

Nonaka, I. and Takeuchi, H. 1995. *The Knowledge Creation Company: How Japanese Companies Create the Dynamics of Innovation*. New York, NY: Oxford University Press. p. 304.

Pangarkar, A. M. and Kirkwood, T. 2013. *Workplace Learning is Not Rocket Science*. Training, 50, no. 6, pp. 80–80.

Patton, M. Q. 2008. *Utilization-Focused Evaluation*. 4th ed. Thousand Oaks, CA: Sage.

Peterson, S. L. 2008. *Creating and Sustaining a Strategic Partnership: A Model for Human Resource Development*. Journal of Leadership Studies, 2, no. 2, pp. 83–97.

Reichheld, F. F. 2003. *The One Number You Need to Grow*. Harvard Business Review, 81, no. 12, pp. 46–54.

Revans, R. W. 1972. *Action Learning – A Management Development Program*. Personnel Review, 1, no. 4, pp. 36–44.

Russ-Eft, D. F. 2014. *Human Resource Development, Evaluation, and Sustainability: What are the Relationships?* Human Resource Development International, 17, no. 5, pp. 545–559.

Schuler, R. S. and Jackson, S. E. 1987. *Organisational Strategy and Organisational Level as Determinants of Human Resource Management Practices*. Human Resource Planning, 10, no. 3, pp. 125–141.

Scriven, M. 1991. *Evaluation Thesaurus*. 4th ed. Thousand Oaks, CA: Sage.

Seddon, J. and Brand, C. 2008. *Debate: Systems Thinking and Public Sector Performance*. Public Money and Management, 28, no. 1, pp. 7–9.

Senge, P. (1990). *The Fifth Discipline: The Art and Science of the Learning Organization*. New York, NY: Currency Doubleday.

Index

OTHER TITLES IN OUR FINANCE AND FINANCIAL MANAGEMENT COLLECTION

John A. Doukas, Old Dominion University, *Editor*

- *Rays of Research on Real Estate Development* by Jaime Luque
- *Introduction to Foreign Exchange Rates, Second Edition* by Thomas J. O'Brien
- *Weathering the Storm: The Financial Crisis and the EU Response, Volume I: Background and Origins of the Crisis* by Javier Villar Burke
- *Weathering the Storm: The Financial Crisis and the EU Response, Volume II: The Response to the Crisis* by Javier Villar Burke
- *Essentials of Retirement Planning: A Holistic Review of Personal Retirement Planning Issues and Employer-Sponsored Plans, Third Edition* by Eric J. Robbins
- *Financial Services Sales Handbook: A Professionals Guide to Becoming a Top Producer* by Clifton T. Warren
- *Money Laundering and Terrorist Financing Activities: A Primer on Avoidance Management for Money Managers* by Milan Frankl and Ayse Ebru Kurcer

Announcing the Business Expert Press Digital Library

Concise e-books business students need for classroom and research

This book can also be purchased in an e-book collection by your library as

- *a one-time purchase,*
- *that is owned forever,*
- *allows for simultaneous readers,*
- *has no restrictions on printing, and*
- *can be downloaded as PDFs from within the library community.*

Our digital library collections are a great solution to beat the rising cost of textbooks. E-books can be loaded into their course management systems or onto student's e-book readers.

The **Business Expert Press** digital libraries are very affordable, with no obligation to buy in future years. For more information, please visit **www.businessexpertpress.com/librarians**. To set up a trial in the United States, please contact **sales@businessexpertpress.com**.